Human Rights Amendments and Constitutional Amends

4th Edition

Proposed amendments to the Constitution of the United States of America and discussion about the proposals.

These modifications are directed towards ensuring the rights of human individuals and limiting both the governments' attempts to restrict those rights and how our elected representatives conduct *our* business.

W. Lewis Collier, Ph.D.

KDP Paperback, 4th Edition, 30 Nov 2025

ISBN 978-1-7321061-8-5

This limitation, of course, does not extend to the verbiage of the proposed amendments. It is, in fact, the hope of the author that many of these amendments will be enacted, thus making the main points of this book free to all.

Contents

Introduction

This 4th edition updates several proposed amendments and add a new one. Prior editions of these writings discussed the courts' reluctance to rule based on what seems to be clearly defined rights. Thus, many of the prior proposals were directed at making those rights crystal clear. This edition adds an additional proposal directed at ensuring the congress also does the job the forefathers expected it to do in balancing the power of the executive and judicial branches.

The new proposal is an attempt to prevent the unfettered incompetence that invaded our democracy in 2025. The number of totally unqualified and crony-driven cabinet members is unacceptable. While the constitution cannot prevent the masses from electing someone who should not be POTUS, save an amendment to prevent those with felony convictions from being eligible for the office, the Constitution must prevent the officers running the country from lacking some modicum of experience and capability in their selected cabinet positions. Congress is supposed to prevent such ineptitude from being sworn into these positions of power. The forefathers never, in their wildest dreams, imagined members of congress shirking their duty as was done in 2025. The Constitution must be updated to prevent congress from consenting to such a travesty of cabinet heads from occupying office.

Introduction to 3rd Edition

This book is a series of draft proposals for amendments to the Constitution of the United States of America, and discussion regarding those proposals. The goal is to provide a framework against which discussion can be held, decisions made, and action taken to return control of the country to the people.

There are two basic themes in these writings. The first is that many "rights" are seemingly and obviously protected within the constitution as it exists today yet are regularly denied by both lawmakers and the courts. Some of these amendment proposals strive to end, finally, these inequities. The second theme is that the rich and powerful have long abused the system to their advantage. Many of the remaining amendment proposals seek to end those manipulations. Along with a few "clean-up" amendments, it is hoped that these changes to the Constitution of the United States of America will truly make us the land of the free, and of equals!

Over the years, there have been several piece-meal amendments that inched towards freedom and equality for all. For some reason, these have never achieved the full intended effect. The "respecting no religion" clause of the first amendment never should have allowed many regulations (e.g., Sunday Blue laws), yet they not only passed through the legislating process but endured scrutiny of the Supreme Court of the United States (SCOTUS). In other cases, women and those older than eighteen years of age were given the right to vote yet no other rights were guaranteed. Even the Fourteenth Amendment, which purports to not "deny to any person within the jurisdiction the equal protect of the laws" has never lived up to its full potential in truly defining that all human individuals are free and equal. It is long past time that the Constitution was updated to reflect what it means, that all are free and equal and that any laws to the contrary, and that apply to one group and not others, are prohibited.

This update is released on the date on which the 47th POTUS takes office. Since the previous edition of these writings, much has happened that seeming should not have been allowed under the constitution as it stands, but they did. As with prior versions, this edition provides updates to stem the tide of partisan SCOTUS decisions that have allowed our democracy to head precipitously close to a full-fledged oligarchy, if not a fascist dictatorship.

President Biden has declared that the ERA is not approved, but this implementation will face multiple legal hurdles. Do states have the right to un-ratify amendments? Article V only says that 75% of the states need to ratify a proposed amendment; there is no proviso for revoking ratification. Accordingly, the constitution has no allowance for setting a deadline for ratification either. Thus, it is up to SCOTUS to decide if the seven-year limit set in the preamble of the ERA is valid. They did so in Dillon v. Gloss (18th Amendment establishing prohibition), and it has been done so for most proposals ever since. Strangely enough, a time limit was *not* included in the proposal for the 19th Amendment (Women's Suffrage).

According to Section 3 of the proposed amendment, the ERA should have become the rule of the land on 27 January 2022, which is two years to the date of the ratification by the 38th state, Virginia. This seemingly foundational change to the governance of the country has received little to no coverage and does not seem to be subject to any significant legal proceedings. One must wonder why!

Regardless of its ratification status, however, the ERA only solves a part of the overall social and economic strife within our country. There are significant portions of our population that are NOT protected by the ERA. This subject is covered extensively later on in the text. Owing to this need, this edition moves the Human Rights Amendment (HRA) front and center, and includes this in the title, to emphasize its importance. This edition extends the HRA to include some other protections aligned to ensuring that living breathing people are protected against governing laws but against effects of deregulated corporate actions. To this end, this edition consolidates the previous human rights proposals into a unified amendment that, when ratified, should provide clear cut protections for *all classes* of humans with respect to legal mandates and corporate greed.

There are other changes as well to the remaining sections. Specifically, even more limits are placed on elected officials since SCOTUS cannot seem to find a requirement for general decency in the current Constitution. Of course it may take a states' convention to ratify these since the status quo has little to no incentive to clip its own wings.

Introduction to 2nd Edition

The writings of the second edition follow the recent SCOTUS rulings that ended, hopefully only temporarily, the right to human autonomy and for well regulation of Militia for keeping and bearing of arms. As such, new amendment candidates are included to address the rights that were gutted by the recent rulings. It still is astounding that the SCOTUS can miss entire sections of the Constitution when taking away the rights of human individuals.

Amazingly, since safe and approved medical care for women is not explicitly listed, then, as stated in the Tenth Amendment, it must be left for the states, or to the people, to decide. Forget the obviousness that our guaranteed right to be secure in our persons, which is explicitly called out in the Fourth Amendment, should include self-autonomy. But I guess not. So, again, the Constitution must be updated to include explicit instructions for seemingly obvious rights to be formally codified.

Yes, the Constitution says that "The powers not delegated to the United States by the Constitution, nor prohibited by it to the states, are reserved to the States respectively, or to the people." But it takes an extreme view to use the Tenth Amendment to overturn rights generally accepted as protected by other amendments. It is this need for such detailed introspection, I believe, that has the country in the crisis it is now in politically. These amendment proposals strive to clearly define and delineate the rights of human individuals, thus rendering the political nature of SCOTUS moot.

In contrast to the overturn of Roe vs. Wade where clearly defined rights were ignored, the current SCOTUS has interpreted the Second Amendment, which clearly says nothing about personal protection, to mean that undefined rights can be included as such. This dichotomy is amazing in its clarion call for reform of the constitution to be more explicit in many cases.

In support of limiting corporate greed, the Necessity Non-Profitability Amendment includes rental housing and education in the list of necessary items to be protected from greed.

We face a serious dilemma if greedy corporations are allowed to own all the housing. A return to the days of owing our souls to the proverbial “company store” certainly will not be too far behind. Rents have outpaced inflation and wages significantly. There is no rational reason as to why rental property owners should reap profits beyond a reasonable return as would be expected should people be able to purchase their homes. And this trend for corporate ownership of “single family” homes leads to pricing out of new homeowners, which leads to an unstable system of rising housing prices that keeps many from obtaining home ownership, or from being able to afford a rental property should their career choice lead to not settling down in a single locale for the entirety of their career. Much reform is needed in this area as wealth in homes is taxed yet wealth in stocks is not. This clearly favors the rich!

The solution to "taxing wealth", however, is not so simple as it may seem. Property taxes generally are collected to pay for local government services. But the basis for such taxes is constructed from value assessments of homes in a municipality. Assuming these values are reasonably accurate across all economic levels, then the tax burden is spread "fairly" between the property owners in a government district. Even in a real estate "market collapse" or "real estate boom", all property values change relatively in sync with others in the area. Thus, the tax burden remains comparatively equal relative to value, or worth. Stocks are not so well behaved. In fact, a mogul could "leak" damming information at tax time to evade taxes, then retract or fix the issue, restoring their wealth. Such a wealth tax would need to account for contrivances such as this to impart fairness.

Finally, wealth itself is a construct of the mind. One can compute their financial "net worth" by adding up their assets and liabilities, but this is ethereal. As noted before, real estate, stocks, and bonds can lose value. Other than hard cold cash stored safely in insured accounts, material items are placeholders for wealth. A more equitable means is needed to generate revenue to run the country.

Income is the metric best used to establish taxes. If a person owns a property and generates true rental income from it, than that is what should form the tax basis. Likewise, dividends from stock, bonds, and savings accounts are taxable, as are the profits from sales of stocks and similar investments. Stocks do not retract dividends. A lack of profits, however, will most likely cause stocks to lose value. And this may even lead to a loss of income should someone sell stock for a lower value than its purchase price. This is acceptable in terms of lowering taxable income. And it is a lot easier to manage the accounting than fluctuating wealth taxation. Do we really want to give back money one year because a stock price dropped? Taxing income from dividends and profit from sales seems to make more sense. And it is a fairer process. Afterall, not only the "founder" who is now worth billions because of the value of their stock is making money. All those who bought and sold the stock, at a profit, made the billionaire so "rich". And when the founder sells their stock, it too will be taxed. Until then, it is just paper.

Education is included in the list of necessities due to the fact that the government took over the student loan business and then decided to try to make a profit from it. Increasing the abilities of the population should have been the goal, not paying down the bill from failed plans such as trickle-down economics. The middle class is paying for trickle down and future generations will continue to pay for it via mounting debt to get an education. This crusade against the masses must stop.

It would seem that the SCOTUS, as it becomes increasingly political in nature, needs to be reined in just as congress needs to be returned to its purpose to represent the people, not to be beholden to special interests. Amendments to rectify these issues are needed more than ever now to preserve our Republic.

The system of governance with the United States of America has also been burdened by improper largess. For too long, politicians and the wealthy few, who often are in the same intersection of class Venn diagrams, have micromanaged the populace via socio-economic engineering and regressive laws to allow for the ruling party to take more control. Control, of course, oscillates with the national mood. These back-and-forth swings of the pendulum have caused America to not move forward as quickly, nor as far, as it should have.

The outcome of enactment of constitutional amendments such as those espoused in this book should restore power to the people and restrict both the government, and our representatives, from holding back the pursuit of the American Dream.

I am an engineer, not a political scientist nor a scholar versed in legalese. As an engineer, however, I strive to solve interesting and challenging problems. My sixty-plus years have enabled me to analyze problems and propose solutions. I also strive, hopefully, to disseminate candidate solutions in an informative way with positive effects. Thus, these proposed amendments are made in laypersons' language, and are accompanied by discussions that further convey the intent of the respective amendments. It is fully expected that the language will need to be altered to meet legal meanings, but these changes should be well vetted to ensure that the underlying intent is not lost.

As an engineer, I also value the meaning of requirements. As such, a constitution serves as the requirements for the running of the country for which the document was written. The Constitution of the United States of America serves the same purpose, but there are gaps in the guarantee of rights for Human Individuals. I cannot say that these proposals close all the gaps, but it is believed that significant lapses in protection will be closed upon enactment of requirements that follow the basic tenets of these proposed amendments. And, if these amendments lack any needed protections, I welcome their addition.

I do not think that these proposals span any political ideology, but others may disagree. The intent is to finally establish that which as alluded to in the Declaration of Independence that all *people*, not just men, are free and equal. As long as capitalistic greed that motivates political actions is allowed, then this freedom will never fully be achieved.

The final wording, of course, would require appropriate Sections, including approval ratification details. The intent here is to present the basis for such amendments and leave the legalese until the full scope is determined.

The book is divided into sections that relate to different areas in which additional protection is seen as needed. The sections below could probably be condensed into a set of six proposed amendments with appropriate sections in each. They are presented separately to allow for more directed conversation and discussion.

The first section introduces a series of amendments that strive to further codify the rights of human individuals. For too long, we have sought to address the rights of individuals in a piecemeal manner. These amendments seek to lay out protections across the board so that we may focus on other issues instead of rehashing and refighting battles that should have been clear in 1776 when those words "All created equal" were written.

The second section seeks to limit the powers of those elected to represent us, we, the people. They are our representatives, and not our leaders. These amendments strive to codify the fact that they work for us, and do not lead us.

The third section addresses issues within the federal judiciary in terms of approval and lack of disparity on the bench. While focusing on the SCOTUS, the actions of both the legislative and executive branches are intertwined in these amendments.

The fourth section addresses changes in how the Executive Branch can conduct its business in leading the country. The President of the United States (POTUS) is effectively the Chief Executive Officer (CEO) of the operational side of the country. As the rules are written now, POTUS has their hands tied when dealing with the legislative branch. These amendments strive to offer a drastic, but necessary, change to the way that We, The People, are governed.

The concluding section includes amendment proposals to return America to the state of respect that was once expected of all denizens of this great country. America was born of Capitalism, but not the unbridled version we have today. These amendments seek to constrain those aspects of our economic system that work for the few instead of the many.

Human Rights

This section is directed towards amendments to ensure the preservation of the rights of human individuals.

Human Rights Amendment

Resolved by the Senate and House of Representatives of the United States of America in Congress assembled (two-thirds of each House concurring therein), That the following article is proposed as an amendment to the Constitution of the United States, which shall be valid to all intents and purposes as part of the Constitution when ratified by the legislatures of three-fourths of the several States within one hundred and seven years from the date of its submission by the Congress:

HRA Section 1: Autonomy Preservation

Section 1. Congress shall pass no law and the Executive branch shall enact no rule that restricts the right of bodily autonomy of Human Individuals who have been born, except when such law or rule is intended to protect a non-insignificant portion of the entirety of all Human Individuals who have been born and/or the global ecosystem at large. Likewise, Congress shall pass laws that do protect the bodily autonomy rights of Individual Humans, as necessary.

This section of the HRA was added to this book after the SCOTUS session ending in June 2022 eroded the essence of bodily autonomy that seems obviously enshrined in the US Constitution. To argue that the Fourth Amendment does not include this right is unfathomable. It clearly says "...secure in their persons...against unreasonable searches and seizures..." The Ninth Amendment states that "The enumeration in the Constitution, of certain rights, shall not be constructed to deny or disparage others (rights) by the people." Clearly this, and the First Amendment say that laws based on one religion that disparage the religion of others cannot stand, yet the overturning of Roe v. Wade certainly does this. This ruling is a trifecta of travesty for what was purported by those who led to the overturning to be "settled law."

This is not a hypothetical situation. Disallowing living and breathing human women the right to decide what happens within their own bodies when they have been criminally violated opens the door to all the other possibilities of criminal violations as well. Doctors have already been found guilty of inseminating their patients with their own semen. With the growth of genetic research, there is no end to the possibilities of gene-matching for nefarious purposes. What is to stop someone from using this personal and confidential data to impregnate a woman to create a body for parts or other material to solve a genetic problem.

With no protection for bodily autonomy, what protection is available to stop this type of action, or to prevent harvesting of the resultant body as well?

The rejection of the "settled law" of Roe v. Wade also opens the door for government forcibly requiring living and breathing human individuals to be forced to violate their bodily autonomy. If a woman, or even a female child, who has been raped can be forced by the government to carry that fetus to term, then what is to prevent others, including the government, from impregnating women in order to create a body for other purposes, such as harvesting organs, or creating soldiers. For that matter, what prevents the government from forcing living and breathing human individuals from donating a kidney, or a cornea, or other transplantable part. Rejection of Roe v. Wade certainly opens a significant Pandora's box of horrifying possibilities.

As with all rights guaranteed by our Constitution, however, one person's rights end when they intersect with the rights of other living breathing human individuals. Given SCOTUS's demonstrated inability to understand this concept, this amendment must be specific in regard to this limit. As such, requirement of administering ordinary and proven safe treatments such as vaccines must be allowed. A total right to bodily autonomy would, of course, enable those who seek it to forgo such treatments, without which the entire population could be at risk. I will not delve into binomial expansion of infectious spread but suffice it to say that every pandemic starts with a single patient zero. The amendment specifically enables the government to enforce statutes that require medical treatments such as vaccinations for diseases that could affect more than just a few people. This, of course, would include conditions such as polio, pandemic viruses, and similar situations. In addition, this Amendment would allow for denial of participation in usual things such as school, public places, and so forth should an individual reject a required vaccine or similar treatment. It is an individual's choice to live alone in isolation should they refuse such things, but it clearly is not their right to endanger others because of their beliefs or fears.

Now for the hard part of the analysis of the effects of this amendment. There is no age limit specified in this amendment, and this is by design. An additional amendment proposal, the Human Age Amendment, covers this. Should there be a situation such as a transgender human individual seeking to alter their status before turning eighteen years of age, this amendment would allow for protection of minor transgender individuals. This autonomy amendment can in no way be construed to limit what is best for the human individual in any condition, including gender identity.

This is not a proposal to allow for gender altering medical treatment in the large. There are, and will be, situations such as being intersex whereby treatment, such as hormone therapy or surgery, is needed by those under eighteen to preserve their overall health. It is up to the individual, their doctors, and their support system to decide what is best for that individual; it is no business of the government to interfere.

HRA Section 2: Class Protection

Section 2. Congress shall pass no law and the Executive branch shall enact no rule that applies to, or affects, any one specific class, or classes, of Human Individuals who have been born, where said class is defined by gender identification (whether traditional male/female, intersex, transgender, non-binary, or other), sexual orientation / preference (whether heterosexuality, homosexuality, bisexuality, pansexual, asexuality, or other), race, color, national origin, medical condition, genetic information, economic status, or other segregation factors, except when such law or rule is intended to prevent discrimination against the Human Individuals represented within the protected class or classes, or to provide necessary protections to a class or classes.

This section runs deep in so many areas! It strives to amplify those protections that the Fourteenth Amendment is supposed to guarantee, but that often are not provided. Those words "nor deny to any person within its jurisdiction the equal protection of the laws" should be enough to stop many of the travesties allowed to continue by lawmakers and the judiciary. This amendment should lay to rest any and all presumptions that "any persons" really does mean everyone!

The intent of this is to enshrine true human rights, that *all* Human Individuals are equal. The Equal Rights Amendment (ERA) from 1972 attempted to make women equal to men, which, of course should be the rule of the land, especially as codified in the Fourteenth Amendment. The ERA, however, did not extend these protections to all human individuals. This section of the Human Rights Amendment strives to do just that. All living breathing human individuals are equal.

This amendment, along with the other amendments, effectively means that the Government cannot enact laws that deal with issues of one sex, gender, sexual orientation, race, skin color, economic status, or other class differentiator over another. Thus, for example, men could not be sentenced to castration for rape. Likewise, limits or restrictions cannot be placed on medical procedures solely affecting men, women, or those who are intersex. These protections extend to all other classes as well.

The "who have been born" clause is meant to exclude those who have not yet crossed the birth canal into open and free space. While there are myriad persons who wish to protect the unborn, that is another matter entirely. As noted before, personal and religious belief systems drive when a human being begins to exist. This expression could be changed to include some form of medical viability to survive outside a womb, but this level of clarification would obfuscate the true meaning of this amendment and is best left to other amendments if needed.

To attempt to hold parents, or solely the mother in the additional case of rape, incest, illegal impregnation by a medical professional, or other such cases, responsible for terminating a pregnancy, or others for performing such a termination, for reasons of the mother's or parents' own deciding, including, but not limited to saving the life of the mother, are clearly not within the purview of any governmental control, other than such services must follow the acceptable standards of all other medical care. Denying this right to self is a significant violation of the First Amendment since such a ban on termination of pregnancies is clearly showing respect towards some religions and not others. This is also a violation of the Fourth

Amendment guarantee of security in their own persons. And, of course, how any such laws restricting personal choice in matters such as medical procedures pass Constitutional muster against the Fourteenth Amendment is a significant slander against the entire system of governance and jurisprudence!

Denial of rights in other cases, however, could be warranted.

All rights guaranteed in the constitution end when actions performed in the name of those rights violate the rights of others. The quintessential example is that of recklessly shouting "fire" in a theater is not protected by free speech since it could result in harm to others. If a woman is pregnant and is planning to carry the fetus to term and the woman and/or fetus is injured or killed by a criminal act of another, (e.g., the mother is shot or stabbed) then the parents have suffered two losses, that of the injury/death of the pregnant woman and also the injury/death of the fetus. As with the concept of viability, protections of this type for the unborn may need to be codified in a separate amendment that covers this specific case. Specialized cases, however, are not the general concept of a constitution, so the ability to prosecute a person who kills or injures a fetus in the manner described in this paragraph should be possible given the current constitution. It is left to legal scholars to comment on the legalese needed to allow for this to happen.

The exception clause "except when such law or rule is intended to prevent discrimination against the Human Individuals represented within the protected class or to provide necessary protections to a class" is provided to allow laws to be made to protect members of a class. The exceptional clause is important as this allows rules and laws to protect members of classes but cannot give one class more rights than others.

The hope, however, would be that no such laws would be needed. With uneven protections within the Constitution, as it stands now, these "hate laws" are needed. But, by codifying strong and all-encompassing Human Individual Rights protection, such laws dictating some killings as "hate crime murders," for example, could be construed to elevate one class above another. Should we penalize someone for violating the rights of another because of the particulars of the human individual whose rights were violated? Again, it is left to legal scholars to debate this, but if all human individuals are truly equal then does violating the rights of one person count as more "serious" than violating the rights of another.

Does the reason for a murder matter to the person(s) left dead by the murderous act?

While not a popular sentiment, killing a Law Enforcement Officer (LEO) may not warrant a more severe penalty all on its own. But given lawmakers' penchant for micromanaging laws down to the type of gun used, I am sure that multiple charges can be brought that would have the same effect in cases such as this without violating the basic principle of the equality of all Human Individuals.

My current belief is that if all human individuals are truly equal then quite possibly, hate laws that add a reason to the original crime (e.g., hate murder) may be past their time. Specific "hate" actions, such as hate speech, which is a form of abuse, should be covered by other laws. Given that we are all equal, then how can we, as a society, justify penalizing some crimes than others based on why the violation was perpetrated? I would suggest that all penalties be sufficient for the crime, regardless of the motive. And, as with the case of causing the death of an LEO, I suspect that the legislature can produce additional laws that would add to the sentence for such vile crimes, again without violating the ideal of equality of all.

The term economic class is included to make sure that those less affluent are not excluded from the equality of rights. A later amendment proposal dealing with taxes and other economic concepts may be unnecessary if equality for all is truly protected. But, following in our forebears' penchant for pointed amendments, this later proposal is included.

A fine point is made regarding the economic class in this proposal deals with taxes. It should be allowed to set a tax rate higher for those earning more than others, as long as the tax system does not apply unequally to those earning more, or less. (In math-speak, the tax rate line could be defined as having a positive slope, meaning those who earn more would be taxed at an ever increasing rate.) Thus, a linear tax rate system that increases the percentage tax rate as income grows would be allowed. Specific deductions for only some within an economic group, based on some exotic criteria such as their industrial basis, would not be allowed.

The above discussion, of course, implies that the slope could be set to allow for a lower tax rate for those with higher incomes. Fine-tuning this amendment to mean that the tax rate must be the same for all earners would be fine by me.

Likewise, so-called "wealth taxes" on those with higher incomes would not be allowed.

The "or affects" clause is intended to ensure that once a law or rule is shown to affect one class more than others then that law also shall be deemed unconstitutional, subject to invalidation or change to remedy the inequality. There are many such cases where this has been shown to be true. From “stop and frisk” laws affecting people of color (POC) significantly more than non-POC to voting restrictions that affect the poor and POC more than rich and non-POC, the list is long both in number and related effects. Existing amendments should prevent these transgressions against rights, but they do not always do so. Laws simply cannot be tolerated when they affect some classes more than others. Thus, should a non-discriminatory law be enacted that is affecting one or more classes than others, or is demonstrated to be so, then such laws are not allowed.

Other amendments are supposed to protect the rights of some groups. The Fifteenth Amendment clearly says that voting laws affecting any class of Human Individuals within a race are unconstitutional. The Nineteenth Amendment gave women the right to vote but did not codify their equal status anywhere else. The Twenty Fourth Amendment protects those who are unable to pay a tax in order to vote. But, again, no other protections were afforded by this amendment. The Twenty Sixth Amendment protected the right to vote for those 18 years of age and older, but again, with no other protections.

It is nigh time that all inequalities in protection of rights be eliminated so that all persons can truly live as equal individual humans.

With all the above, it may appear that affirmative action laws and policies would be forbidden, but this is not a certainty. Laws to protect classes are explicitly allowed for just this reason. A litmus test, using college admissions as an example, would be along the following lines: Policies that seek to equalize benefits across classes would be allowed. This would have the effect of allowing colleges to normalize acceptance criteria across the applying classes. The details would have to be worked out, but in concept, the grade point average (GPA) could be statistically analyzed so that the same percentage of whites and POC would have the same opportunity to attend an institution. Not the use of the word "opportunity". This does not mean that the acceptance and student body makeup must match the general population. The acceptance and student body must by in sync with the applicant pool relative to the general population.

HRA Section 3: Individual Priority

Section 3.Congress shall pass no law and the Executive branch shall enact no rule that provides benefits to the government or to any corporate or other similar entity beyond those benefits provided to Individual Humans. Likewise, Congress shall pass laws that do protect Individual Humans from Corporations and similar entities, including the Government itself.

The intent of this amendment is to ensure that individual human beings are equal to, or above, corporations or other entities, including other forms of government. The term "Individual Humans" is used instead of citizens to explicitly state that this applies to all people, not just citizens. This follows from the wording of the Fourteenth Amendment that extends the protection to "any person within its jurisdiction." All persons are deemed to be equal or above corporations.

The effect of this amendment is to codify that corporations are *not* humans. Owners of corporations are protected from consequences of their actions by a "corporate veil" so they should receive no better benefits from society than do individual humans. And it would seem that corporations indeed should have less, and certainly no more, protection than individual humans.

This does not, however, protect corporations and entities from rules that do not affect human individuals. For example, corporations have completely different tax codes, rules, and rates, which could be different than what human individuals pay for the same level of income. As guardians of human individuals' lives and careers, corporations also need significant restrictions on what they can do in that their actions that affect Human Individuals with little to no consequence.

This amendment covers many other areas as well. One clear-cut example is the ability for corporations to lobby government officials and spend significantly more than individuals for attempting to direct laws and rules towards their benefit. This amendment prohibits such dealings as the rules and laws, as currently enacted, clearly give benefit to corporations over individuals. Lobbying as a career would simply cease to exist. Companies can write letters or call the representatives from their home state, just as Human Individuals must do, instead of using their vast capacity of largess to tilt the field on their own behalf.

Another place where this amendment applies is in tax laws regarding savings and other comparable items related to employment of individuals. As an example, those who work for businesses are enabled to save more with deferred taxes than are self-employed individuals. Employees of companies can direct more of their earnings into 401K plans than can an individual (e.g., self-employed) into their respective IRA plans. This clearly is a benefit to corporations as individuals are incentivized to work for a company rather than themselves in order to reap the tax deduction. Individuals should have no limitations placed on their financial decisions just because they do not work for a corporation.

Another major example is health insurance. Corporations are handed a golden goose when it comes to the well-being of their employees. Laws that stifle self-ownership of health insurance (until we implement a one-payer system, of course) are detrimental to Human Individuals. Numerous times, people have been forced to stay at a job because of the health insurance. This needs to stop. Humans should not be enslaved in this manner to the sole benefit of corporations.

Other areas are numerous, but also worthy of a brief discussion. One such issue is that businesses can choose the status of benefit taxation that benefits them and not the employees. That corporations can choose to have disability benefits, even when premiums are paid for by the employees, to become taxable benefits is unfathomable, just to save the corporation a few dollars in its own taxes. Businesses can also deduct multiple expenses, including relocation and moving expenses, yet Human Individuals are not allowed to claim many of the same deductions. This list goes on and on, all hurting the majority of Human Individuals whilst allowing a select few, via the corporate shell, to benefit from the losses of the majority. This feature of current laws is so inherently un-democratic, it is amazing that it has been allowed to exist. This amendment strives to eliminate these inequalities.

Many will argue that such "benefits" are necessary to enable businesses to grow and to provide economic job creation and growth. I would counter that degrading and limiting Human Individuals should never be used as an excuse for laws and rules. So called "trickle-down economics" have been repeatedly shown to not flow wealth to the masses as is claimed. Laws supporting this lie are to be banned.

The second part of this amendment is again aimed at something that is not common in the Constitution. While several existing amendments state that "The Congress shall have power to enforce, by appropriate legislation, the provisions of this article." there is no direction to do so.

This part actively directs Congress to enact laws to protect human individuals (and, of course all as a group and not just individually) against corporate misdeeds that negatively affect human individuals. The list goes on, and on, and on, forever, of course. A few, but by no means a complete, list of protections to consider include things such as protection of personal data, medical history, and other information that can be used to undermine the other rights guaranteed within the Constitution.

As we continue along in the "Internet Age," the ability to learn intimate details about all human individuals grows continuously. Congress must be directed to pass laws that prevent both companies and the government from taking advantage of the liberation of our information freedom to be used against us. Europe, for example, is doing this, America should as well!

And do not even get me started about the potential perils of artificial intelligence.

The environmental protection laws also fit squarely within the protections to be guaranteed by this proposed amendment. As I originally composed this amendment, SCOTUS had again weakened environmental protections. Never, ever should corporations be allowed to do anything that hurts the environment needed by all Human Individuals, and, in fact, all living things that make up the ecosystem of planet Earth. Again, Congress is actively directed to continue to protect our rights to a safe environment.

HRA Section 4: Punishment Limit

Section 4. Congress shall pass no law and the Executive branch shall enact no rule that enables a penalty more severe than life imprisonment with no chance of release from said imprisonment.

The intent of this amendment is clear: punishment by death shall be eliminated. Human individuals are infallible as both jurors, prosecutors, and yes, even as defenders. In all cases, error in human actions where the death penalty is to be served results in a non-retractable sentence that is to be forbidden. To prevent such mistaken sentencing, the penalty of death should no longer an option in the USA.

To those who quote "eye for an eye" from a religious source, then the First Amendment should surely preempt such attempt to respect one religion over another. The true meaning of the ancient "eye for an eye" quote is unclear; it often is interpreted to not demand equality in punishment for the crime. Even Jesus said to turn the other cheek. Conflicting "rules" from the same religious-based artifact clearly cannot be used to direct laws and punishment in the USA.

Discussion could go on and on, but we, as human individuals, simply cannot be trusted to use penalty of death as a punishment, much less as a deterrent.

HRA Section 5: Defense Safeguard

Section 5. Congress shall pass no law and the Executive branch shall enact no rule that restricts the rights of Human Individuals who are defending their innocence for any crime, even after having been found guilty of the charged crime. Likewise, Congress shall pass laws that do protect Individual Humans from the behavior by the government in terms of being questioned regarding or prosecuted for a crime.

The intent of this amendment is to ensure that there are no limits placed on the ability of a human individual to defend themselves when charged with a crime, even after having been found guilty of a crime. There are an incredible number of cases whereby prosecutorial misconduct, defense representation incompetence, and judicial bias have resulted in people being found guilty of a crime, or even multiple crimes, of which they were innocent. The sheer number of "Innocence Projects", and their corrective rate of more than 2 of every 5 cases, demonstrates this clearly!

There simply cannot be any limit placed on the right to defend innocence related to time constraints, procedural missteps, or any other issue related to denying freedom to those wrongly charged or convicted. The penalty of some who truly are guilty of their crime who are abusing the legal system cannot be used as an excuse to keep innocent people incarcerated.

The second part of this amendment is aimed towards something that is not common in the Constitution. While several existing amendments state that "The Congress shall have power to enforce, by appropriate legislation, the provisions of this article." there is no direction to do so.

This part actively directs Congress to enact laws to protect human individuals (and, of course all as a group and not just individually) against the government and its agencies regarding questioning regarding and prosecution of a crime. Far too often, "confessions" are coerced by those seeking a guilty party rather than determining the truth or "guilty" verdicts are expected from a biased jury.

Specifically, to this point requiring a safeguard, laws must be passed and enforced to ensure that all interrogations are fully recorded visually and audibly for the entirety of the sessions so that any such malfeasance by the questioning agency may be detected. As expected, this means that such confessions or other statements during such interrogation sessions shall not be admissible should they not be fully recorded and preserved. Many states now have laws "on the books" regarding this. This practice must become the law of the land to ensure that the right to liberty is not hindered due to improper questioning tactics.

There are myriad other similar cases, but explicit enumeration should not be required to support the need for the rights protected by this amendment.

Human Taxation Amendment

Congress shall pass no law and the Executive branch shall enact no rule that causes human individuals with lower incomes to pay relatively more than human individuals with higher incomes in taxes, tolls, and other levies on items needed for sustainable living.

The protections provided by this proposed amendment should be covered by Section 2 of the proposed HRA but given the inability of SCOTUS to read basic English language, this point is repeated here, just to be sure. Hopefully the HRA sections are clearly defining of the rights they guarantee, but just in case, this and other proposed amendments are included. Since this amendment is strongly associated with the socio-economic aspects of the HRA, it is included in this section.

The goal here is to eliminate all taxes and tax rates, tolls, and levies, and similar economic charges that affect lower income individuals disproportionately more than those with higher incomes. This protection is essential since these encumbrances are a larger percentage of the overall income and ability to pay of those who earn less. For example, fuel taxes, sales taxes on general necessities, tolls on roads traversed to earn an income, and the like, take a larger percentage out of the lower income pockets than they do out of higher earners. Thus, it would be expected that all such levies would be consumed by the overall income, and possibly property, tax rolls so that those who can have, earn, or own more pay more towards the societal good.

This is not a call for a flat tax, but, rather, for a system whereby those who have more income (whether active or passive) pay at least as much, relative to income, as do those who earn less. A flat tax rate would be the minimal solution, but this amendment does not preclude a tax rate with a positive slope that results in higher earners paying at a higher percentage rate than lower earners.

Note that this amendment constrains the socio-economic aspects of the HRA. It is left to the experts to fine-tune the wording, but the point remains: The many cannot be made to pay for all that is needed for the few to become rich! Making workers pay tolls to drive to work so the owner can become rich is unfair. The public ways should be paid for based on return to the individuals.

This amendment also would eliminate the Social Security and Medicare deduction caps for high wage earners, as this benefits higher income earners. It would be expected that if all income were included in these deductions, even at a flat rate, then the rate would decrease, thus benefiting lower earners even more. This explicitly is to be allowed under the realm of this proposed amendment!

This amendment also would cause introspection of the wealth of individuals. Lower income folks who pay an annual tax on their capital possessions (e.g., a house) should not be unfairly burdened when others are allowed to grow non-physical capital assets with no annual tax burden.

A system whereby all aspects of income are taxed at an equal percentage for all persons is to be invoked.

The "items needed for sustainable living" clause, however, does not mean this equity applies to non-essential "vice" items such as alcohol and tobacco. Anything that is not essential for life is subject to extra taxation. Items needed for valid medicinal purposes, however, even if for items normally identified as a vice (e.g., cannabis) would not be subject to such taxes when needed for medically approved purposes. And certainly, products needed for one gender versus the other, e.g., feminine hygiene products, would not be subject to such taxes.

Human Age Amendment

Congress shall pass no law and the Executive branch shall enact no rule that applies to any age group, to the exclusion of others, over the age of 18 years after birth, except when such law or rule is intended to prevent discrimination based on the ages represented within the protected class or to provide necessary protections to a class, regardless of years of age after birth.

The aim of this amendment is to ensure that there are no age-related rules such as purchasing certain products (e.g., alcohol) or attendance of legally sanctioned venues (e.g., casinos). These currently are mostly restricted to those 21 years of age or older, yet 18 years of age is the legal voting age. This amendment effectively supersedes the 26th amendment by enshrining *all* rights to those who have reached the age of eighteen, not just the right to vote. This mitigates the issue where those who fall within the range of 18-21 years of age are too small a block to affect their own destinies, despite their right to vote. No group should ever be in this position regardless of age or other classification.

This amendment, however, is meant to allow for protection of members of an age group, such as is done now for older workers.

There will be those who deride this as enabling drunk driving or consumption of dangerous tobacco products, but that is not the intent. Society has seen a significant increase in awareness of the effects of these products and, in general, their usage and related effects have decreased. But to say that the increased age limits solely led to the decreases is unfounded. At the same time as the legal drinking age was increased, a large awareness program was also instituted. It is unclear whether the reduction in incidents is not partially due to increased training.

In any case, it is unfair to ask human individuals to go fight in wars, and to allow them to vote, yet not be able to enjoy a product enjoyed by others whom they defend. The proper solution is continued awareness of the dangers of such products and proper enforcement of laws against driving under the influence. And, of course, the government should continue to promote healthy choice and to strongly advertise the dangerous effects of all such legalized vices.

This amendment is also meant to allow for laws and rules to protect those under the age of 18 years of age from birth, such as child labor laws.

Representatives

This section provides amendment topics that constrain actions and operations of those elected to represent We, The People.

Representative Restraint Amendment

Congress shall pass no law and the Executive branch shall enact no rule that provides benefits to themselves beyond Individual Humans, with the sole exception being for protections afforded to POTUS, other duly elected or appointed representatives, and their respective family members as required to ensure national security. All such currently existing benefits beyond normal situations are to be eliminated and reverted to a common set of benefits commiserate with the societal norms for such benefits.

The intent of this is to ensure that our government representatives do not enact rules for themselves that do not also apply to non-government representation individuals. For example, congress has given itself gold-plated medical coverage and retirement plans yet do not offer the same to individuals. While this should be covered in the proposed Human Priority Amendment, this is meant to specifically ensure that government representatives do not vote for themselves benefits above those provided to the individual humans.

This would have the immediate effect of eliminating all the rewards given by the legislators to themselves, such as better retirement plans, medical coverage, and the like. In addition, their raises would be no more than those given to government programs such as Social Security.

This amendment, however, is not meant to totally eliminate pensions and other post-service benefits (e.g., secret service protection for ex-POTUS and family). The goal is that the benefits should be in line with those provided in general to human individuals in general.

Representative Business Amendment

The U.S. Senate and U.S. House of representatives shall conduct all business with simple majority votes of members present constituting a quorum required for conducting business, except as noted elsewhere in this constitution and shall neither pass nor follow any rules that prevent conducting normal business due to non-essential constraints.

The makeup of the senate and congress was strategically and purposefully set to provide equal representation of the states in the senate and of the people in the congress. Any rules set by the senate or congress bodies themselves that change this, such as the filibuster, deny equal representation. Only in those cases specifically outlined in this constitution, which were done so with deliberate intent to ensure decisions needed to be made by a significant plurality, shall be decided by more than the simple majority. And it should be clear that those decisions (e.g., a guilty finding for an impeachable offense) shall not be altered from what is specified in the constitution by legislative bodies.

This amendment specifically is not intended to affect decisions based on population. That is, votes are by member of the chamber and are *not* weighted by the number of persons being represented by the representative. This amendment, however, will help prevent representation of a minority of the population to hold the democratic process hostage via non-simple plurality processes such as the filibuster.

Finally, congress shall not enact nor follow rules that prevent conducting normal business for non-essential reasons. The recent lack of progress in the House of Representatives because of the dysfunctional leadership party should not cause all other business to cease!

Representative Districting Amendment

All members of federal and state legislature bodies (US Senate, US Representatives, and State-level legislatures) shall be chosen by and represent a district that is determined by a published methodology that imparts geographical closeness of those represented instead of ad-hoc boundaries.

The intent here is to prevent gerrymandering. Odd-shaped districts set by human individuals' interests instead of a politically agnostic algorithm, are not to be allowed when selecting representation areas for US or state-level congresses. Rather, geographical relationships of those represented are to be used to shape districts. This follows from "closeness" algorithms whereby rational district constituency boundaries are generated by population numbers only instead of race, socioeconomic, or other factors. Making the algorithm publicly available will ensure that there are no secret agendas hidden within the voting districts. This, of course, means that voting districts cannot be manipulated to have the same effect as is now done with gerrymandering.

This is also intended to improve representation. Elongated and grossly odd-shaped gerrymandered districts cause extremely disparate district membership. With such manipulated representational districts, a district can range from one metropolitan area to another with minimal residents in the middle. Clearly those in one metropolitan area may have different interests than those in the other metropolitan areas and those in the thinly populated middle region. Closeness algorithms will cluster those represented into more geographically centered regions, where common representational needs should exist.

Judiciary

This section provides amendment topics that shape how the federal Judiciary branch is operated.

Judiciary Representation Amendment

The SCOTUS shall be made up of a set of justices, each of whom represents each of the circuits that shall be comprised of geographically adjacent states and territories. Nominees by POTUS must currently serve within the same federal circuit as the outgoing justice represented, or at the state level for one of the states or territories within the circuit. Congress may change the number of circuits, but this number must be odd.

The intent is to have geographically diverse and regional representation in the SCOTUS. Justices, once confirmed, are now assigned to serve in alignment with the judicial circuits. There is no requirement, however, that they be versed in the regional matters over which they preside. SCOTUS should not be packed with "Washington insiders," as is often the case; it should be staffed with a diverse populating that truly represents the overall USA populace and by persons who are knowledgeable with the affairs of the region for which the represent on the SCOTUS.

The adjacency clause means that each circuit needs to be comprised of states and/or territories that are geographically similar, as is done now with the circuits. It is envisioned that a circuit could be formed that includes the territories, but it may be better, for example, to include Puerto Rico and the US Virgin Island territories in a Southeastern US circuit and Guam in the circuit that includes Hawaii. As with the federal judicial experience requirements proposed later, this is left to Congress to define.

Of course, the odd number is a requirement for ensuring there are no ties when cases are decided, assuming all justices vote. Recusals, medical issues, or other absences could lead to such a tie but the court itself should be charged with devising a methodology for preventing such issues. And, if these amendments are adopted, it is hoped that many issues become “no-brainers.”

Judiciary Leadership Amendment

The Chief Justice of the SCOTUS shall be designated as the justice with the most tenure following the death or retirement of the previous Chief Justice.

The intent is to have POTUS nominate new associate justices, from the circuit region of the outgoing justice, and to have the currently serving and remaining justice with the most experience lead the court. As the lead justice of SCOTUS, it is imperative that the Chief Justice have considerable experience residing on the SCOTUS bench, rather than being politically motivated.

Time served should count for something for SCOTUS justices. Setting the direction of the court based on experience seems to be a good thing. I must say that, in general, Chief Justice Roberts has presided well in his term, but is it best that he had to learn that role as well as learning how to be a justice at the same time?

Judiciary Experience Amendment

SCOTUS nominees shall require at least ten (10) years of judicial experience, as defined by Congress, at the state or federal level.

Federal court judicial nominees shall require at least five (5) years of related judicial experience, as defined by Congress, at the federal, state, or local level

Extensive relevant experience is needed to be a federal judge. In both cases, it is up to congress to fully define this experience, in terms of what counts towards related judicial experience, but the expectation is that someone with only a few years of judicial experience, whether as a judge, prosecutor, attorney general, or similar role simply does not have the requisite experience for deciding cases presented to the SCOTUS.

This experience provision will, I believe, lead to the desired turnover of SCOTUS justices. Having jurists that are over fifty years of age, which should be the norm given the experience requirements, should allow for shorter terms overall, leading to more opportunities for adding new justices over time.

There has been a drive to impose term limits, but this is a fool's errand. Most proposals for limited terms to the SCOTUS are based on an expectation at a new justice would be needed every two years (which is unreasonable unless starting from nothing). The thinking is that each POTUS would get to appoint two justices every term. But this approach is fraught with peril! Life-time appointments are the only reasonable way to ensure that justices will not be killed or otherwise coerced into retirement to ensure that the sitting POTUS and an aligned senate would not pack the bench.

Finally, it is hoped that the SCOTUS caseload will lessen given the protections of these proposed amendments. As alluded to before, the protections should be more straightforward given clarification and expansion of rights within these proposals. If a law results in affectations to a class, then it is unconstitutional. The hope is that the decisions become much less political and much more straightforward, thus lessening the SCOTUS political underpinnings.

I am not a legal scholar by any means, but it has always amazed me that these huge decisions seem to rest on just one part of the Constitution. In Engineering, competing requirements need to be vetted against each other to ensure that a correct solution is provided. The more recent trend of trying to apply literal interpretation of one part of the Constitution, with total disregard for the other parts that explicitly guarantee some rights, needs to stop! It is hoped that having more experienced justices and federal judges will stop the inane and politically motivated rulings.

Judiciary Approval Amendment

SCOTUS nominees shall require a two-thirds majority of the full Senate for approval and a three-fourths majority of the full Senate for removal.

Federal court judicial nominees shall require a three-fifths majority of the full Senate for approval and a three-fourths majority of the full Senate for removal.

If the Senate fails to begin deliberations of any judicial nominee presented by POTUS within 30 days and fails to hold a final confirmation vote within 90 days following presentation of said nominee then consent shall be deemed to have been given, unless nominee is presented within 90 days before an election day where nominating POTUS is up for reelection, is ineligible for reelection due to limits of this constitution or has been found guilty of impeachable actions.

The intent is to require a supermajority so that judicial nominees will be impartial and not severely leaning towards one political ideology, unless two-thirds of the Senate is controlled by a similar ideology (God help us all). Likewise, it should take three-quarters of the Senate to remove a SCOTUS justice.

The intent of the final clause is to prevent congress from stalling on judiciary nominees, except when the current POTUS is up for removal from office as noted.

This brings into question of whether a sitting POTUS would be impeached just to prevent them from nominating someone. The wording clearly states that the POTUS must have been found guilty, and obviously not removed from office nor barred from running again because of that impeachment. I have to trust that the POTUS will not be impeached every time a SCOTUS justice replacement is needed!

Executive

This section provides amendment topics that shape how the federal Executive branch is to be operated.

Presidential Veto Amendment

Congress shall pass no law that cannot be vetoed in part by the President. All laws shall be specified in such a manner that entire sections, subsections, clauses, or other legal partitions, down to an individually specified rule or law may be vetoed by the POTUS while accepting all other segments of the bill or provision. Likewise, Congress must override any individually vetoed section, subsection, clause, or other legal partition, down to an individually specified rule.

The intent of this is to provide POTUS line-item veto power. Congress has far too often piled so called "pork" into bills or added non-related items. The intent of this amendment is that each bill will be directed towards a specific topic, with the understanding that multiple laws and rules can be passed together, but the POTUS can veto the "pork," or other aspects of the law which are found to disagree with the administration's goals and objectives.

The same override rules will apply to vetoed line items as currently apply to entire bills that are vetoed. That is, each vetoed item must be overridden individually, and not as a complete package.

Presidential Pardon Amendment

The President shall have the power to grant Reprieves and Pardons for Offenses against the United States, except for himself, family members, or business associates; in Cases involving harm to multiple Human Individuals; in Cases of Impeachment; in Cases of Insurrection against the United States; or for members of his staff during his time in any office at the federal or state level.

The intent of this is obvious. POTUS cannot use his office to pardon those who did his bidding as members of his staff or family. Nor shall POTUS be allowed to pardon anyone convicted of crimes against the state while committing acts of insurrection against the United States.

I would love to be able to add in a limitation to the most recent pardons by POTUS 47, but I am at a loss as to how this could be worded. It is inconceivable that the US spends what it does, and acts as it does, to prevent drug trafficking then pardons drug dealers.

The 4th edition adds the clause "in Cases involving harm to multiple Human Individuals" but I am not sure this is what is needed. Surely someone convicted of dealing in drugs would fall into this exception, as would someone polluting, etc. But I feel that this clause does not completely capture the needed limits on pardons.

Federal Elections

This section provides amendment topics that shape how the federal elections are to be operated.

Federal Office Qualification Amendment

Section 1. Except when running for re-election as authorized by this constitution or when VPOTUS seeks to succeed the POTUS under which they serve when the previous POTUS' term is limited, no candidate for federal office or congressionally approved position shall hold another elected federal office during the election or selection cycle.

Section 2. All candidates for federal positions (POTUS, VPOTUS, SCOTUS, Senate, Congress, and all positions requiring Congressional approval) shall not be convicted of any crimes greater than a misdemeanor or that prevent travel to any foreign countries.

Section 3. All candidates for elected federal positions (POTUS, VPOTUS, SCOTUS, Senate, and Congress) shall not have lost a prior election for the same office.

The intent here is to prevent people from holding on to their present elected office (e.g., congressperson or senator) and, at the same time, also be running for another office (e.g., POTUS or VPOTUS, senate, or congress) or to be a candidate for an appointed position (e.g., cabinet member, leader of a federal agency, or other positions requiring approval of congress).

Oddly enough, this seems to be already covered in Article 1, Section 6, of the US Constitution, but it is not. Senators are moved into Cabinet positions, so it is assumed that they officially resign their elected office before being sworn into the Cabinet. This amendment would hasten the time in which they need to resign their elected position in order to be a candidate for such a position.

Being elected or appointed to serve as a representative or other leader should be the job undertaken. If one wants to seek another office then they certainly may do so, but the people they represent or the government department they serve deserve full-time representation, not part-time service as their federal representative or leader seeks another office.

While in free enterprise, human individuals are allowed to look for a new job whilst holding on to their current position, this should not apply to our representatives. Being an elected representative is an honor and unique position. There are only an exceedingly small handful of such positions compared to the overall population of those gainfully employed in the country. To allow holders of these positions to double dip is not rational. The opportunity to serve must be opened up to all who desire to serve as much as possible. This proposed amendment does this, and it should help eliminate many politicians from making careers out of "serving" their fellow Americans.

This, of course, does not apply to those seeking re-election for the same office, within the limits placed elsewhere within the Constitution. Thus, POTUS and VPOTUS may run for reelection as can congressional or senatorial representatives. And VPOTUS can run for POTUS while serving as VPOTUS. In the odd chance that VPOTUS assumes the POTUS position (e.g., death of POTUS during the election cycle) then VPOTUS would be allowed to continue running for POTUS.

This amendment proposal, however, does not seek to impose term limits on members of congress. Congressional staffers already manage an incredible amount of the representational effort. It is posited that term limits could hinder government by actually shifting even more power to unelected staff members. It is expected that turnover within the ranks of congress would be encouraged by other amendments so that representatives as lifers would not be so prevalent.

Section 2, of course, needs to be added since we have POTUS 47 that has been convicted of multiple felony counts. This alone would prohibit him from being a service member, yet he is commander in chief of all armed services. This travesty of justice is inane, at best, and utterly embarrassing to the country, especially since POTUS 47 is not allowed to visit 38 countries at the time of his swearing in.

Section 3 may be a stretch but if someone loses an election at the federal level, they should not be allowed to run again for the same position. The political parties do not have the foresight to make this distinction when selecting candidates, so the Constitution must provide this guidance.

This protection may seem pointless, but it has happened in the past. Grover Cleveland, and now POTUS 47, are the only two Presidents who have won reelection after losing their reelection bids. There have been a few who lost an election then ran again and won (Reagan and Nixon are most recent examples). In order to keep a fresh lineup of candidates, those who have lost an election need to step aside and let others run.

Federal Popular Vote Amendment

The POTUS and VPOTUS shall be elected as a pair of human individuals based on receiving a majority of the popular votes of entitled human individuals across all states and territories and shall be allowed to serve no more than two terms in each role, regardless of how they came into the position.

This does away with the electoral college, which has many faults and is rooted in historical deals to form the union when slavery was allowed. This institution needs to be eliminated and this amendment does so.

This also helps restore a true balance of power between the branches. States elect the Senators and Representatives. For the states to also be so influential in election of the POTUS means that the people, as their own entity, are not as well represented as they should be in the Executive branch.

This lack of representation of the People in the Executive branch also matters when it comes to the third branch, the Judiciary. This amendment, and the Judiciary Representation proposal would help spread judiciary representation as is needed.

There are many who say that this amendment should also contain a provision for ranked choice voting. This method of voting is purported to encourage growth in the number of parties by allowing candidates from alternative parties to have a chance at winning, and thus undoing the blockade of the two-party system.

I am not in disfavor of such a voting scheme, but I do not yet believe that it alone will lessen the power held by the two mega-parties that we have today. I do feel, however, that many of the other proposed amendments will, however, force whoever is elected to follow the will of the people and not corporations and greed.

The final clause of this proposed amendment would limit the number of terms that any one human individual can serve in each position of POTUS or Vice-POTUS. Being elected as POTUS more than twice is already limited in the Twenty Second Amendment. But a more literal interpretation of the Twenty Second Amendment could present a loophole.

The wording in the Twenty Second Amendment leaves open the possibility that a person could be elected as VPOTUS, with the plan that the elected POTUS immediately resign, letting one who had already served twice as POTUS serve an additional term in the position. Those who would usurp the intent of the Twenty Second Amendment clearly would have no trouble using this loophole to maintain their control and effectively become a dictator. This must not be allowed.

Age requirements also could be addressed by this amendment but currently they are not. Article II, Section 1 addresses a minimum age, but no maximum age limit is specified. Given that many of our current POTUS and candidates are approaching the expected life expectancy for their generation leads some to say there should be an upper limit as well. While I agree in principle, I feel that just as SCOTUS should not have a retirement age, neither should POTUS. It is left to the American Citizenry to elect those who they feel can best serve the country and its needs. If a partnership between POTUS and Vice-POTUS meets those needs, then so be it. Experience has its benefits, limits on age could prevent that experience from being used to help the country.

Federal Succession Amendment

Should the POTUS and VPOTUS be incapacitated or die at the same time, their vacancy shall be filled in the following manner.

(1) The two willing and longest serving members of the Senate with the same party affiliation as the incapacitated or deceased POTUS and VPOTUS shall immediately assume the duties of POTUS and VPOTUS until replacements have been selected as defined below. Should there be a tie for tenure then preference shall be given to Senators from the same state as POTUS and VPOTUS, or geographic closeness.

(2) The Senate shall, within three (3) calendar days following the vacancy, nominate at least three (3) and no more than five (5) Senate members who meet the requirements to serve as POTUS and with the same party affiliation as the incapacitated or deceased POTUS and VPOTUS.

(3) The House of Representatives shall vote within three (3) days of the Senate making the above nominations, using

rank choice voting, for a replacement POTUS and VPOTUS.

(4) When one candidate has a majority, that person shall be deemed to serve as POTUS and the person with the second most votes shall be deemed to serve as VPOTUS and shall serve until the POTUS or VPOTUS is no longer incapacitated or, in the case of death, until their term expires.

(5) Should POTUS return from being incapacitated, the person selected by the House to serve as POTUS shall serve as VPOTUS and the person selected by the House to serve as VPOTUS shall return to their duly elected position within the Senate.

(6) Should the VPOTUS return from being incapacitated, they shall assume the duties of POTUS, the person selected by the House to serve as POTUS shall serve as VPOTUS and the person selected to serve as VPOTUS shall return to their duly elected position within the Senate.

(7) Governor(s) of the states from which the selected Senators represent shall appoint replacements with the same party affiliation as those selected to serve as POTUS and VPOTUS to serve as Senator until the replacement of POTUS or VPOTUS is no longer needed, or until the term of the Senator expires.

The goal of this amendment is to get someone serving immediately, regardless of any political battles going on in either chamber. This proposal also specifies how the replacements are to be selected within the framework of the Constitution instead of being left to devises of the Congress itself.

The immediate need for a replacement POTUS and VPOTUS drives the first clause. This is not, however, without risks and challenges. Senators with the longest tenure often are incredibly old and not up to the challenge of serving as POTUS or VPOTUS. Thus, the "willing" clause attempts to have Senators not up to the challenge refuse the offer to serve as POTUS. This, of course, relies on the common decency of such long-tenured Senators to "do the right thing" and take themselves out of the running, hopefully even before a need arises.

This tenure aspect, of course, reaches into other areas of the Constitution. To prevent the issue of tenure and age from arising here, the qualifications for POTUS itself could be constrained to a maximum age. Term limits for Senators, if enacted, could also create issues since there could be multiple Senators with the same tenure given term limits. Specificity of such details leads to unintended consequences. These need to be ironed out to prevent a situation whereby replacements cannot be easily decided. This is the goal of the closeness of states wording, but other options are available.

This amendment also preserves the party affiliations of all affected positions and fills both positions quickly in order to resume normal operations of the country while minimizing impact on the democratic process. Current succession rules, which are not enshrined in the Constitution, rely on a functional House of Representatives to have a duly elected speaker. This, of course, means that a different party could find itself in power in a dual vacancy. The people overall elected a party, as well as people, to lead. Allowing the death or incapacitation of both leaders to swing control is not to be allowed. And, as has recently happened, having a Speaker of the House is not a guaranteed thing. This amendment seeks to bypass this possibility should the need arise.

This amendment also speaks to the nature of House and Senate elections. Since both occur at the state level, having replacements from either chamber gives favor to states over the people at large, which is the intent of the Federal Popular Vote Amendment. Having the POTUS replacement be subject to more immediate (every two years) whims of a state seems to be less suitable for a longer-term position such as POTUS or VPOTUS. Thus, specifying that replacements come from the

Senate seeks to impart a slightly longer-term flavor to the replacement positions.

Federal Voting Rights Amendment

Congress shall pass no law and the Executive branch shall enact no rule that affects the voting rights of any class of citizen based on their income, residence location, or any other protected classification. Likewise, Congress shall pass laws that do protect Individual Humans from disruptions to the voting process.

The goal here is to prevent any voting rules or restrictions that affect one class more than another. The Fifteenth Amendment should already protect this right, but there seems to be something about the Fifteenth Amendment that does not hold the sway that it should. As with many of the prior piecemeal amendments, the limitation to protections "on account of race, color, or previous condition of servitude" does not appear to be a wide enough net.

Voting rules and regulations must not affect one class more than any other. If a voter ID is required, then access to such required IDs must be equally available to any and all eligible voters. Thus, closing ID offices in rural areas, which imparts a higher burden on those voters, should not be allowed. Likewise, having too few ID offices or even the means of casting ballots, in an urban area such that long waits are required also should not be allowed. That the judicial rejection of these seemingly "no-brainer" unconstitutional laws has not happened means that a more encompassing amendment may be needed.

Other parts of the constitution already prohibit poll taxes and the like. This amendment would extend those protections of the right to vote to any and all forms of hardship to any class of voters. If having a single election day means citizens cannot vote without having to take a day off, then other measures, e.g., mail in ballots, early voting, drop-off boxes, a voting holiday, and the like, must be enacted to preserve their right, and ability, to vote.

At the same time, such measures must preserve the sanctity of the vote. While voter fraud is often claimed to be widespread, the fact is that fraudulent voting is rarely an issue or is often perpetrated by those who claim it to be rampant. However, ballot collection frauds, destroyed ballot collection boxes, and other violations of the sanctity of the vote all serve to both dissuade voters and cause disruptions in a fair and fee election. Rules and laws seeking to prevent this level of fraud are allowed as they do not target, nor do they disenfranchise, any one class of voters.

Note that this protection clause includes all Human Individuals, not just citizens of the United States. This amendment is about protecting the right to vote, not defining who gets to vote. Since non-citizens do have the right to vote at some levels, they are not to be excluded by these protections.

Federal Election Funding Amendment

All elections at the federal level (POTUS/VPOTUS, Senate, and House of Representatives) shall be funded by the US Treasury. Congress shall make the rules to be followed in terms of funding limits, eligibility qualifications for candidates, and campaign periods, but no funds may be used more than one (1) year before the election of POTUS/VPOTUS nor more than six (6) months before a senate or congressional election day. These campaign time limits shall also apply to any organization when their primary purpose and of their expenditure is towards the election of candidates. Advertisements and other pronouncements from campaigns funded with federal money shall only state what the candidate for whom the artifact supports will do, shall not be misrepresentative in nature, and shall not be negative towards other candidates.

These incredibly long campaigns for federal representative positions need to end. Coupled with the limits on officeholders seeking another office, this amendment should reduce the national fatigue of these elections. Organizations not formed solely to advance candidate(s) (e.g., F.O.P, unions, and similar non-political groups) clearly can exercise their freedom of speech, subject to any other limitations enjoined from the Constitution, but no earlier than the given time limits.

The mudslinging also must cease. Ads by candidates must be focused on what the candidate will do and not attack the other candidates. In addition, all statements must be clearly defendable and not be a misrepresentation of the candidate's position. Examples of such misleading ads include things such as saying they support a position when, in fact, they are on record against the position or have voted for the position because it was bundled in a bill that had other things supported by the candidate. In the case of changing support, the ads must clearly denote the change in stance and explain why the position changed.

Discussion of this proposed amendment could continue forever, but the point is this: stop the inaneness of long and disparaging campaigns and spend the time representing the people instead of trying to drum up money for the next election cycle.

Miscellaneous

This section provides amendment topics that cover miscellaneous items.

Human Protection Amendment

The second article of amendment to the Constitution of the United States is hereby repealed and replaced by the following:

Congress shall pass no law and the Executive branch shall enact no rule that restricts the right of human individuals from keeping and bearing arms for purposes approved by congress, such as hunting game or fowl for food, target practice shooting, or, for protecting, from non-self-initiated threats, themselves, their families, their property and possessions, or, as a part of a well-regulated law enforcement agency or US Government Military service, the United States of America and protecting its resident human individuals from enemies of the country, provided said human individuals can demonstrate competency, capacity, and commitment to follow rules regulating the safety of use, handling, and storage of such arms.

This proposed amendment actually expands gun ownership rights from what is stated in the Second Amendment. Protection of self, family, and property is explicitly enshrined in this updated version of the right to bear arms; it is *not* in the current second amendment!

The Second Amendment is another one of those Amendments in which guaranteed rights have been severely overextended by the courts. With an initial phrase that many say clearly defines the intent, especially coming out of the Revolutionary War that was fueled in part by the banning of individual gun ownership by the King, security of a free State, against outside aggressors, was the intent. A textualist could easily say that this Amendment, in fact, does not even allow for private ownership for hunting or self-protection. A free state would have to include self-protection in some fashion, which it clearly does not given the introductory phrase about a well-regulated Militia.

This is an amendment that clearly needs to be restructured from the top down. Protection clearly is meant to follow the definition whereby the gun owner and bearer did not start the trouble, as is often ignored in "stand your ground" laws. Use for recreational purposes such as sport shooting are also included. This amendment also includes the right to bear arms for law enforcement and military service, which matches the second amendment's

Militia clause. All the things that second amendment proponents espouse are included. Likewise, all the restrictions on gun ownership and possession desired by many proponents of "gun control" are also included.

The explicitness of this amendment addresses the need for assault rifles as well. Obviously, law enforcement and military service uses would allow for high-capacity magazine weapons, but there could be other applicable uses as well. For instance, protection of property might include the need for such weapons for fending off varmints and critters attacking livestock or feed and grain stores. A swarm of rabbits, or other such animals, threatening a food-supplying farm might only be eradicated with rapid-fire weaponry. This, of course, would be subject to regulation to prevent anyone from owning a high-capacity weapon without a demonstrated need. Even then, the permission to use such a weapon might need to be limited to a seasonal deployment based on the threat. If lawmakers can determine other legitimate uses for high-capacity weaponry, then they can add it to the list. But outright ownership of such weapons of mass destruction is not a guaranteed right.

The only limit placed on the right to own and bear arms is an explicit requirement for rules and regulations, as was obviously intended in the

Second Amendment's "well regulated" clause. Any weapon must be stored, overseen, cared for, and, of course, used, in a safe manner. Those who own and bear arms need to demonstrate the capability to use such weapons in an appropriate manner.

As for where the right to bear arms exists, that is a much harder point to ponder, and to restrict. Obviously, guns would need to be transported, in a well-regulated manner, for non-protection uses. Carrying guns, even target pistols, to practice ranges and target events would, of course, be subject to regulation. Separation of firing pins from weapons, and ammunition from the weapons might be viable ways to minimize danger during transportation. Transporting hunting rifles to hunting areas, similarly, would follow regulatory guidance. The elephant in the room, of course, is concealed or open-carry for protection.

Large capacity weapons, of course, would not qualify for self-protection in an open environment so they, appropriately, would not be allowed for open or concealed carry. As stated above, they might be needed in a more secluded setting, such as on a farm, but fending off a swarm of varmints out in public is not to be expected, thus rifles of any kind, and shotguns, in general, would not be suitable for open carry, except as part of law enforcement or homeland defense. Smaller and limited capacity arms, such as pistols, could be considered for self-carry.

Since the purpose for smaller arms is for self-defense, the decision for open or concealed carry is complicated. An open holster with a six-shooter might be seen as a deterrent but it could also be considered as a threat, thus the intent of protection versus attacking may be clouded by the open display. Further discussion of these limitations is needed to clarify this area.

It is left to the legal beagles to devise the final wording, but the intent should be clear: ownership and the bearing of arms come with restrictions based upon demonstrated capability, skill, and competence.

Necessity Not-For-Profit Amendment

All essential care, utilities, resources, rental housing, education, and all services and amenities required to safeguard the health and well-being of human individuals shall be subject to not-for-profit rules, as enacted by Congress.

Healthcare professionals (doctors, nurses, caregivers, and the like) should, and must, be paid proportionately, and appropriately, for the service they provide to other humans. These practitioners have dedicated their lives to caring for others, spent years of studying to become certified, and continue to educate themselves on the latest treatments and care provisioning techniques. For them to not be rewarded for their sacrifices is unjust.

We, however, simply cannot continue to allow for billions and billions of dollars' worth of resources to be diverted to line the pockets of greed. Layers of management, paper-pushers, and approval-gatekeepers of necessary care, which did not suffer through the long hours of schooling and day-to-day efforts to provide professional care for those in need, should not be rewarded on the backs of the caregivers and patients.

Medical care used to be not-for-profit in the sense that it is today. Doctors worked all week, taking Wednesday afternoons off for golf (at least some did) and we paid well for *their* efforts and dedication to caring for the human condition. Those with the drive and desire to care for others need to be rewarded but not at the expense of those who need care. Having layers of regulations that dictate prices paid based on having insurance cannot be allowed to continue. Policies that allow company-insured patients to pay less than those without insurance would be disallowed from the Human Priority Amendment, but, as we have seen, we need to be specific to make sure our voices are heard.

Likewise, all necessities for human well-being such as, but not limited to, power (petroleum, natural gas, electricity, and all other forms developed forthwith), water, rental-housing, and education should not be run as for-profit entities that are subject to the whims of investors and money-making endeavors rather than providing necessary services to the populace. The lack of care of electrical equipment and facilities in California and Hawaii that lead to massive wildfires, the total break-down of the isolated electrical grid in Texas during the ice storms of 2021, and the lead disaster in Flint, Michigan's water supply, all in the name of greed, should serve as reminders that both Democratic and Republican leadership put profits over essential services. Greed has also encroached upon the rental housing market. Industrial property management companies seek inordinate profits from the present tenants instead of long-term growth from capital investments. The student debt debacle has sapped the ability to prosper from more than a generation of human individuals. And the drain continues, even with the US Government running the student loan program. Education for general prosperity and the betterment of humankind should be the goal, not paying down the debt resulting from poor policies.

Our country simply cannot move forward when basic services are not as efficient and safe as can be due to lining the pockets of greed.

This amendment, however, does not preclude a solid return on investment in essential services (except educational loans). There was a time, before deregulation, when utilities were considered to be a safe investment because of their almost guaranteed rate of return on revenue. This surely is a satisfactory way to run those services upon which the country depends. This also provides a relatively safe haven for investment for those with less wealth who cannot afford to gamble in the speculative market that the stock exchanges have become.

And since when is it a good idea to sell our national grid or major food producing companies to a foreign country? Most recently, the sale of a major steel production company was blocked. Where was this common sense when selling off other assets needed for the growth and security of the country?

This amendment does not address this specifically, but it is hoped that by eliminating greed from the equation, that ownership of these assets necessary for our national security could be brought back to our shores.

Fairness Doctrine Amendment

All reporting, except as in articles clearly identified as opinion or parody pieces, shall be fair and unbiased. Any outlet not subscribing to this amendment shall not be allowed to call itself a news organization and is not subject to the protections granted under the First Amendment or other parts of this Constitution.

The fairness doctrine must be reestablished. All the talking heads claiming to be news can still have their pulpit, but these cannot be called "news." Radical left-leaning and right-wing organizations that serve to make money and stir up public sentiment over truly fair and balanced reporting of noteworthy events, weather, and sports cannot be allowed to even use the "NEWS" moniker.

True news providers must be protected from the threat of frivolous lawsuits for reporting the truth. Those who spout mistruths and propagate lies, however, should have no such protection and should be held accountable for their pronouncements when such events cause harm to the national good.

Conflict Of Interest Amendment

All candidates for POTUS/Vice-POTUS, Federal representatives and congressionally approved appointees, including cabinet members and SCOTUS, shall submit full and unredacted financial records, for themselves and their immediate family members, for examination by Congress before announcing their campaign, before being announced for an appointment or nomination consideration, and shall, within 90 days of taking office, have all financial instruments, other than their primary residence, whether owned by themselves or their immediate family members, placed (with no penalty for such conversion) into a "blind-trust" during their time in office, and shall receive no compensation for any outside activities during their time in office.

The time has come for all representatives (POTUS, VPOTUS, SCOTUS, Senator, Congress, and those whose appointments are approved by Congress) to put the interests of the human population of the country before their own personal gain. The aim is that anyone running for a federal position will submit all pertinent financial records at the time of their announcement of intent to run for a federal office. Those nominated for congressionally approved positions, including justices for federal courts, would submit their financial records at the time of vetting for such approval.

Once elected or appointed, such persons would have ninety calendar days in which to divest their holdings in any and all instruments that could be swayed to loss or gain by actions of the government.

This amendment also would include elimination of any compensation for book deals, speaking engagements, or other such activities during their time in office. Their job is to represent people and not to line their own pockets from their time in office during their time in office.

It should be clear that this may limit the "participation" by those who have amassed an entangled fortune that is not easily unwound. It could be posited that these are not the people we want running the country. Millionaires and billionaires who want to use their wealth to exert control are not what is needed to lead the country. If true leadership is their pure goal, then they should have no issue following the rules set forth by this amendment. There are, of course, sufficient persons within the country capable and willing to serve within these constraints so that we are not beholden to those with massive wealth accumulated upon the back so of working-class Americans.

Honors Amendment

No person who has conspired against these United States of America, who has failed to take action to quell any uprising against these United States of America, has resigned in disgrace from public office, or who has been convicted of, and not pardoned from, felonious crimes or high crimes and misdemeanors may be honored by having any public entity named after them nor shall they be entitled to any other honors as may be normally entitled.

This amendment speaks to how we honor our public figures. Numerous military bases were named in "honor" of confederate leaders who led an uprising against the United States. It is a long and dark history lesson as to why these people were "honored" and it is satisfying to know that much, but not all, of those doings were corrected, just to be "un-corrected" by the current administration. Still, it is worth noting that history often repeats itself so this amendment strives to prevent those actions from happening again.

Competency Amendment

All persons nominated for a position that requires congressional approval, or to hold any position that affects the well-being any person, world-wide, or the safety and security of the United States, shall be well-qualified to hold the position to which they are nominated. The qualifications shall be defined by congress and approved by POTUS not less than two years before application to a nominee, and may not be changed wholesale once the base qualifications are established.

This amendment calls for nomination and approval only of well-qualified persons to cabinet and related leadership positions. These enactors of the will of the people, as determined by the laws and budget passed congress, must be suitable for the job at hand. It should be understood that those in charge of the various Departments should be well versed in the associated field, not those with minimal experience in executing programs on the scale of a US Government Department. There is no need to procrastinate about the current slate of cabinet leaders.

While this treatise cannot address all qualification definitions, a general discussion can be provided. Nominees for these important leadership positions *must* be very experienced in the respective area of their position. Defense positions might be expected to have experience of, or equivalent to, career officers reaching the rank of Officer-Level 6 (O-6), which equates to full Colonel, in most service branches, or Navy Captain. Health and education nominees would be expected to have a similar level of experience, which is nominally 20+ years in the field. Other cabinet and related positions should be defined as having similar levels of experience. And, since these positions lead significant organizations, the qualifications should also include suitable leadership experience as well.

It is well understood that these qualifiers will limit the number of suitable nominees; that is exactly the intent! Those with just on and off again service in a field simply cannot be allowed to run a cabinet department. And, most certainly, those with absolutely *no* experience in a field cannot be allowed to run or have a major position within these organizations. In the 250 years of this country, there have not been any times where no qualified cabinet leaders could be found. I am sure that not all were the best qualified, but certainly I suspect that in no time in history has the cabinet been led so ineffectively.

There are other positions that will need to have qualifications listed as well. The position of Ambassador to a foreign country comes to mind. These are sometimes handed out as political favors but should not be. I'll leave it to the foreign policy experts to define these qualifications, but I would like to think that an Ambassador is at least fluent in the language of the country to which they are assigned.

The qualification timeline within this proposed amendment strives to prevent a congress that cow-tows to party over country from changing the qualifications to serve the wants and desires of a current POTUS. As with many of these proposed amendments, change cannot happen immediately. But, assuming that if a rational set of qualifications are approved then congress is prohibited from changing them for immediate purposes. The exact wording of this likely needs to be reviewed but the goal is that congress cannot update the rules for immediate application to nominees of the current POTUS' choosing.

Made in the USA
Monee, IL
13 September 2026

62981948R00075